Ransom Reading Stars

Astronaut
by Stephen Rickard

Published by Ransom Publishing Ltd.
Unit 7, Brocklands Farm, West Meon, Hampshire GU32 1JN, UK
www.ransom.co.uk

ISBN   978 178591 840 7
First published in 2010
This revised edition published 2019
Reprinted 2024

Copyright © 2019 Ransom Publishing Ltd.
Text copyright © 2019 Ransom Publishing Ltd.
All photographs courtesy NASA/JPL.

A CIP catalogue record of this book is available from the British Library.

All rights reserved. No part of this publication may be reproduced, stored in a retrieval system, or transmitted, in any form or by any means, electronic, mechanical, photocopying, recording or otherwise, without the prior permission of the publishers.

The right of Stephen Rickard to be identified as the author of this Work has been asserted by him in accordance with sections 77 and 78 of the Copyright, Design and Patents Act 1988.

ASTRONAUT

Stephen Rickard

LIFE AT THE EDGE

Ransom

The Space Shuttle Orbiter

Main engines. There are three.

Wings. Used for takeoff and landing. Not used in space.

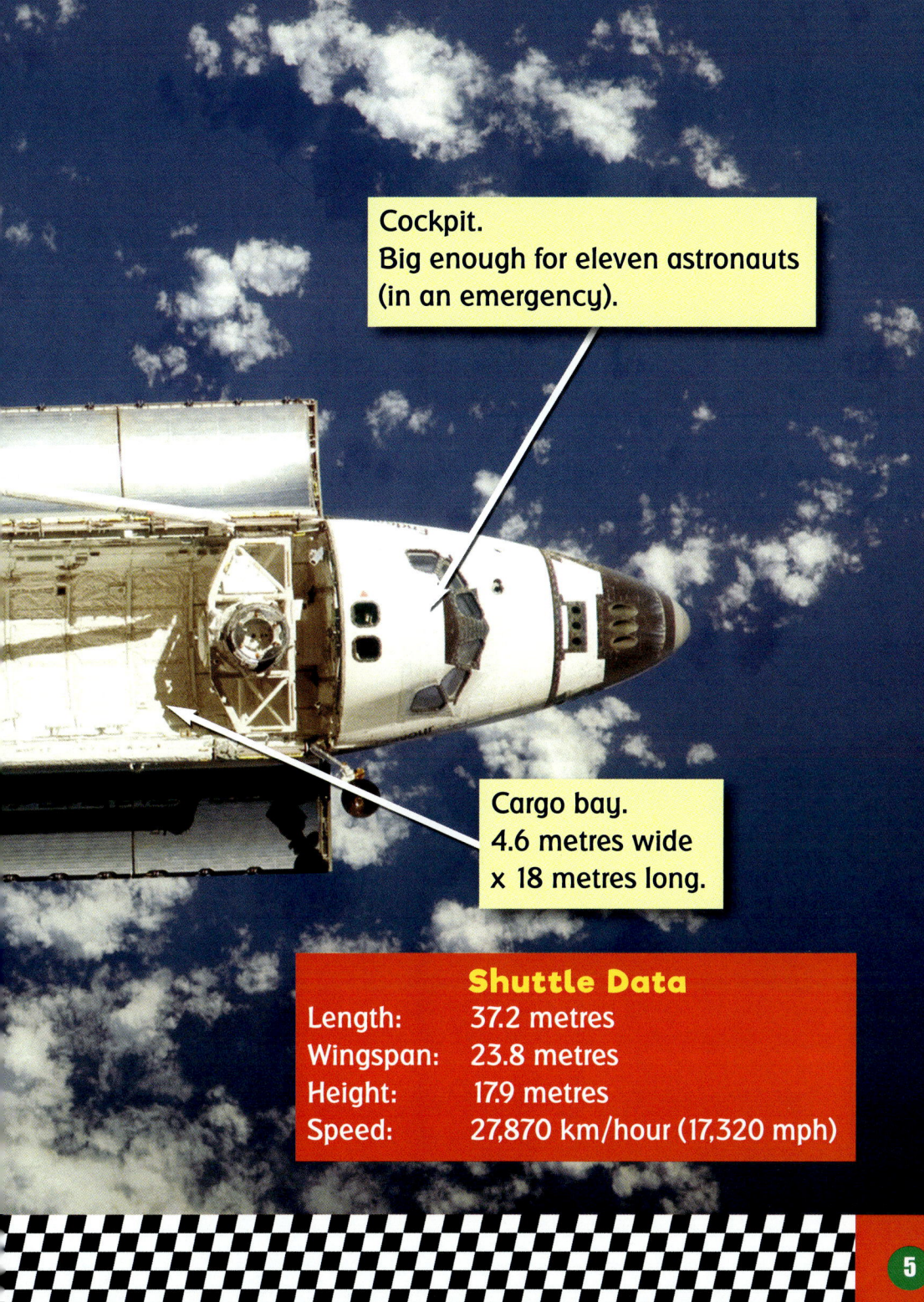

Cockpit.
Big enough for eleven astronauts (in an emergency).

Cargo bay.
4.6 metres wide
x 18 metres long.

Shuttle Data
Length: 37.2 metres
Wingspan: 23.8 metres
Height: 17.9 metres
Speed: 27,870 km/hour (17,320 mph)

The Shuttle was built at the Vehicle Assembly Building, three and a half miles away from the launch pad.

Then slowly it was moved to the launch pad. That's called the rollout.

Here you can see the rollout.

You can see the launch pad in the far distance.

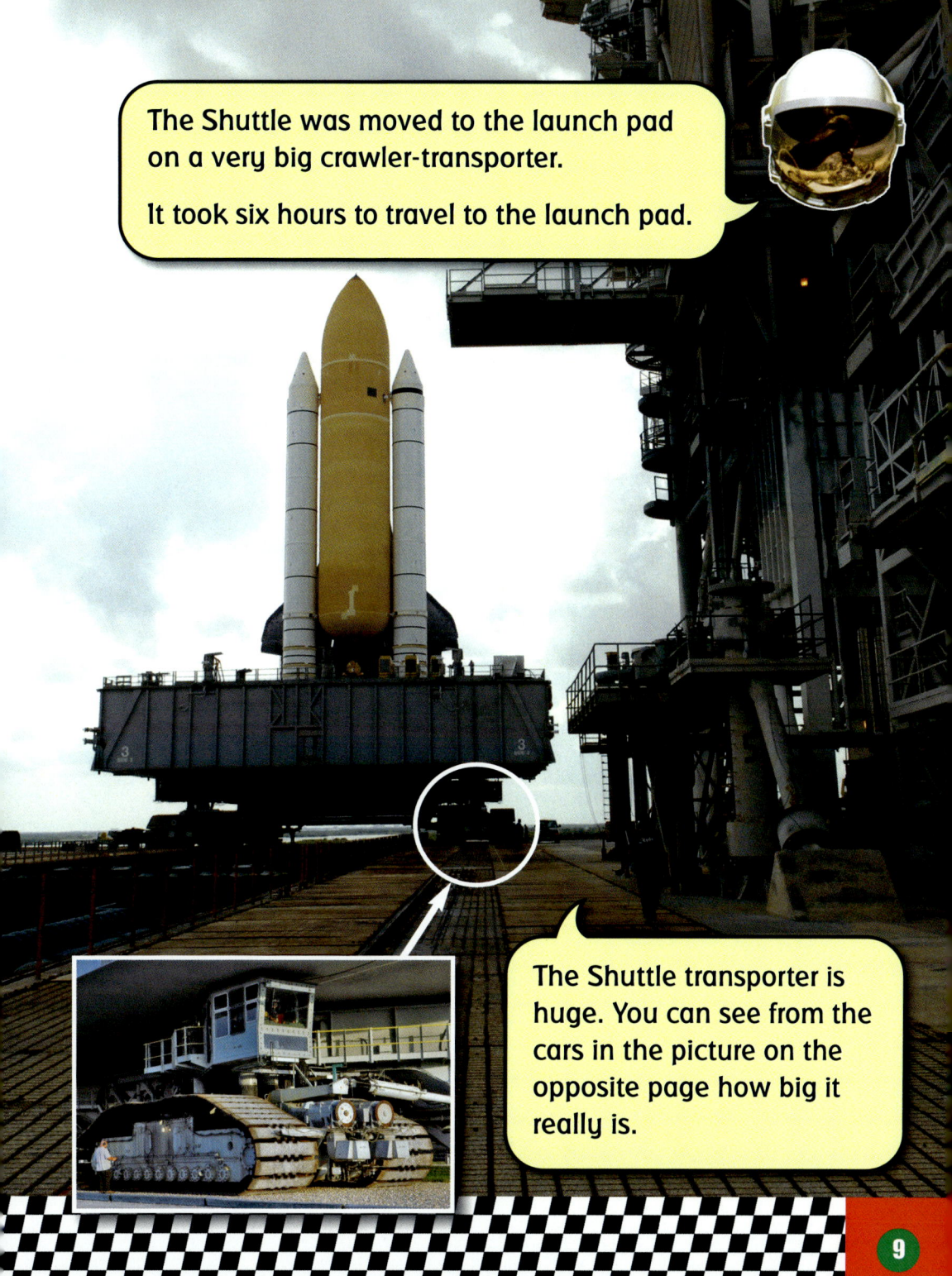

The Shuttle was moved to the launch pad on a very big crawler-transporter.

It took six hours to travel to the launch pad.

The Shuttle transporter is huge. You can see from the cars in the picture on the opposite page how big it really is.

But now the Shuttle is ready for us. This is for real.

The big orange tank is full of fuel. This fuel is very cold.

It is so cold that it makes the fuel tank shrink as it is filled up. I can hear it creaking as we get near the Shuttle.

The Shuttle has three engines. The big orange tank has the fuel for them.

The two big white tubes next to the orange tank are called solid rocket boosters.

They are extra engines. They give extra power for lift-off.

It's now three minutes before launch. We call that **T minus 3**. The engines start to power up.

T minus 31 seconds. The Shuttle's computers take control of the launch.

T minus 6 seconds. The three main engines fire up. Three seconds later they are at maximum thrust.

Everything is shaking like crazy.

T minus zero. Launch.

The boosters ignite and explosive bolts release the Shuttle. We have lift-off!

We feel a big kick as the boosters fire. The noise and the vibration is almost too much to bear.

T plus 45 seconds. We break the sound barrier. We have gone from 0 to 1,234 kilometres per hour in 45 seconds.

Now everything is shaking even more.

Less than a minute later we are travelling at more than three thousand kilometres an hour …

… at an altitude of 20,000 metres.

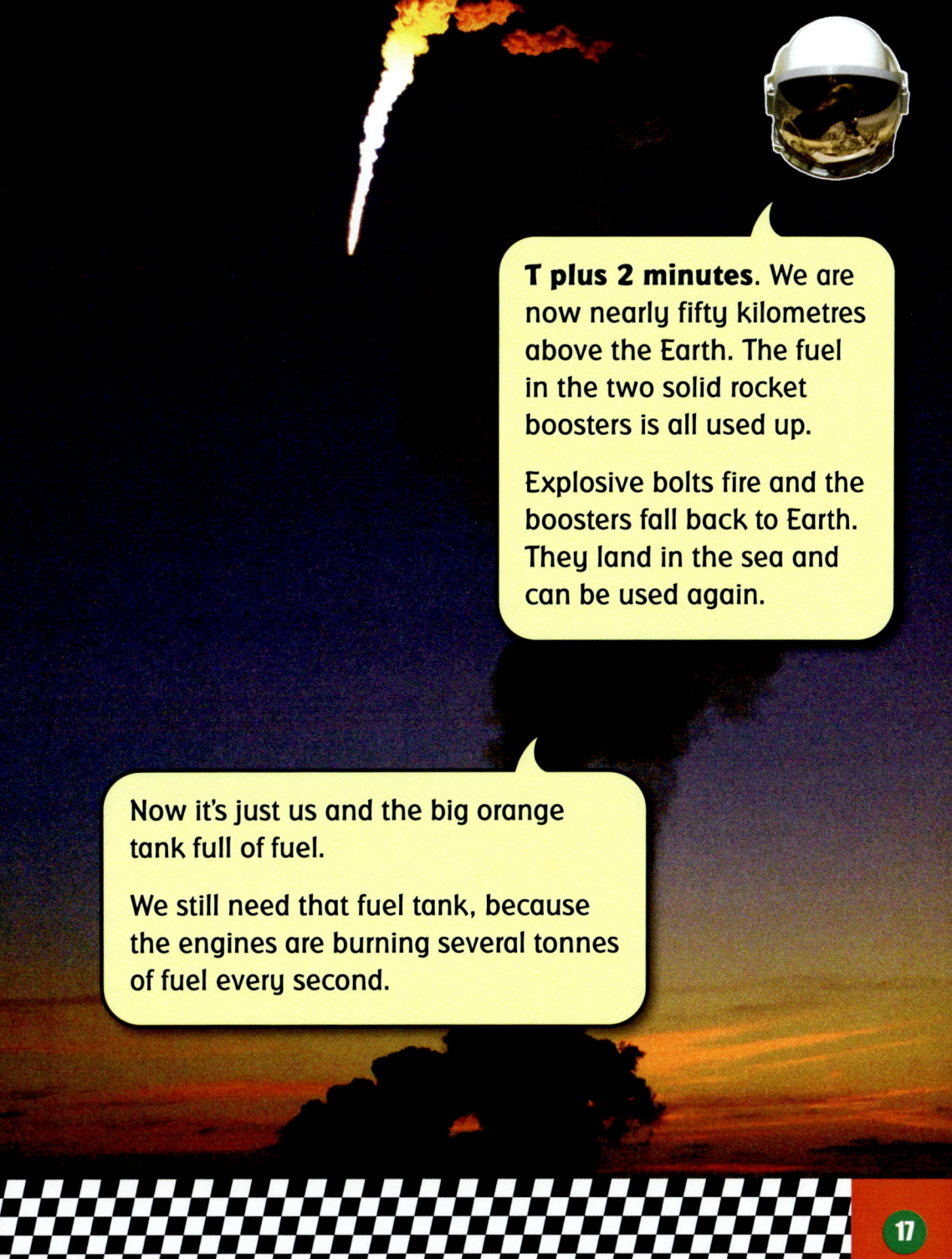

T plus 2 minutes. We are now nearly fifty kilometres above the Earth. The fuel in the two solid rocket boosters is all used up.

Explosive bolts fire and the boosters fall back to Earth. They land in the sea and can be used again.

Now it's just us and the big orange tank full of fuel.

We still need that fuel tank, because the engines are burning several tonnes of fuel every second.

T plus eight minutes. Just eight minutes after launch, and we are in orbit around the Earth.

Now our big orange fuel tank is empty. We don't need it any more, so we release it and it falls back to Earth.

Most of it will burn up as it enters the atmosphere. The rest lands in the sea.

There is no gravity in orbit, so when I undo my straps I float across the cockpit. Now we are really in space.

We take off our suits and helmets. We can wear normal clothes inside the Shuttle.

We are orbiting about 320 kilometres above the Earth. We are travelling at more than seven kilometres per second, which is about 17,000 miles per hour.

But it doesn't feel as if we are moving at all. The shaking has stopped and everything is quiet and calm.

This is the inside of the shuttle. We call this the mid-deck.

You can see that it's all a bit messy.

It looks beautiful, but space is a hostile place for people.

If I was outside without my space suit, I'd live for just 15 seconds.

So the Shuttle and my space suit are keeping me alive.

This is the flight deck of the Shuttle. We call it the glass cockpit.

There are 11 computer screens.

Keeping stuff tidy on the Shuttle is really hard. Everything keeps floating out of the drawers.

So we always end up stuffing things in bags and holding them down with bungee cords.

This is where we sleep. We don't call it a bed – we call it a sleep station.

We sleep standing up, except of course there is no "up."

29

Don't forget – we're not on holiday. We are here to work.

Sometimes we have to fix other satellites. This is the International Space Station (ISS for short). The Shuttle comes to visit it now and again.

Sometimes we have to go outside to fix things.

We call that extra-vehicular activity, or EVA, for short.

Can you see the astronaut fixing the outside of the ISS?

Here is the Shuttle with its cargo doors open.

We usually carry about 22,000 kg of cargo. It might be food for the ISS, or spare parts.

We also take the rubbish from the ISS back to Earth.

This picture was taken from the International Space Station.

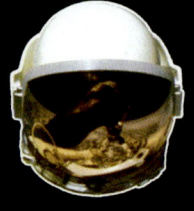

This is how we see the International Space Station from the Shuttle, as we move away from it.

It looks like a giant metal insect.

Then, twelve days later, it's time for us to go home.

But that's really another story.

Jargon Buster (word list)

altitude
astronaut
Astrovan
atmosphere
bungee cords
cargo bay
cockpit
crawler-transporter
engine
extra-vehicular activity (EVA)
glass cockpit
gravity
hostile
International Space Station (ISS)
Kennedy Space Centre
launch pad
mid-deck
NASA
orbit
rollout
sleep station
solid rocket boosters
Space Shuttle Orbiter
spare
thrust
Vehicle Assembly Building
zero gravity